JELLY WAS THE WORD

JELLY WAS THE WORD

DONALD L. WEISMANN

Foreword by Roger Shattuck
Introduction by William Arrowsmith
Photographs by Il maestro ignoto di Firenze

1965   :   Pemberton Press   :   Austin

for those who lost

FOREWORD

It's a big country. Transportation and communication have pushed us to the point of calculated frustration where no one can live anywhere anymore. You just ooze across the intervening spaces, stuck to the traffic and the commercials. Pity the hindmost. Pity the foremost. Remember we're living what intelligent foreigners consider to be the vision of the future. But they cannot tell you what happened to the present; having lost it, we alone can find it. Here it is. It never gelled just this way until an American painter type in Italy for a year blew these limber lines out his nose flute and showed them around. He had stood off just far enough to see and hear.

Still, Donald Weismann made a tactical blunder. Instead of leading with a certified ten-syllable professional fad-word (e.g., surexistenomenolosophism) or a new undergraduate four-letter slogan (e.g., fick, shut), he opted for five limp letters with no jail record, no awards or fellowships. Worthless copy. Does he really expect anyone to hear? That of course is the point. The whole point. Several carefully selected New York editors failed the test. What do you do then when you bear the responsibility of being "the one with the word"? You short out the established literary shunting circuit and openly produce a clandestine book.

In one of those compact collections of scientific essays for laymen, there's a piece about "colloid and crystal." No question, the mileage in those two terms will carry author and readers through their remaining years of office. But they also allow us to grasp the brilliance of Donald Weismann's blunder. *Jelly* is indeed the word. It means that flat fishbelly surface we used to use for printing programs and menus and poems in multicolored inks. It means swollen cheese-cloth udders dripping the juice that will finally set in jars, then transformed by a white wax crust into miniature skating rinks. It means the plain grey tube that preceded the pill. It means the roll that eased jazz into a library and even a congress. It means the fragmentary folk dialectic—" 'cause jam don't shake like that." So it must be jelly, even if no one around will hear of it.

(I had better complete the earlier thought. The term paired to jelly, like colloid to crystal, stands firm by the gastronomic cosmology. *Thin hot soup.* There you have the two states of matter that hold and bathe us. In the fulness of time, life came up from primeval gruel. Jelly formed later when things began to cool out. At the very back of his shelf of tapes Donald Weismann keeps a reel of sounds recorded he will not reveal how or where. He confided one night after a violent dart game that the reel holds the opening of his next long poem. Only the first few noises are recognizable—and barely—as words. "Soup, he burbled . . ." Or gurgled, or gargled.)

I don't know where Donald Weismann was born and blew his youth, though I know such things about a lot of less interesting writers who are not painters to boot. I figure the place must lie just short of midway between Kentucky and Denver, in a war-surplus automotive junkyard kept by a bibliographer of slang and song. But anyone can extrapolate. Just now—a sturdy well-set now—he occupies a high bluff west of Austin overlooking the greater part of Central Texas. Altitude, you understand, suits both his voice and his vision. From that vantage point commanding a landscape of warning sirens and radio and TV broadcast masts, the word wafts out gently rocking the airwaves. That's Donald Weismann in his studio, composing with screwdriver, sablehair, glass negatives, and taperecorder.

Jelly, he says. Let us play.

—Roger Shattuck

Lincoln, Vermont
July 1965

INTRODUCTION

Donald Weismann is a painter of *virtù* who has now turned his unpredictable hand to verse. If he had been content to write the usual amateur's verse, modish and well-mannered, no preface would be required. But this is not the case. Weismann's verse is, like everything he does and is, *sui generis,* unmodish and unpredictable, a fresh farrago of wit, rage, high-bar rhetoric, and good seriousness, written almost as the man himself talks—which is unlike the speech of any man I know, livelier and more graphic. This is rare indeed, and needs mediation. For it is not to be expected that an unknown poet who writes a poem called "Jelly was the Word" and publishes and illustrates it himself in Austin, Texas, is apt to get an audience even as far away as Amarillo. But a man "with the word" should somehow be heard.

What then is Weismann up to? In a word, jelly-making. And jelly, as the poem tells us, is "the fated everlasting force that winds and binds absolute and relative in wordless space and time." In short, a poem of the Logos according to Weismann: "In the beginning was the Word, and the Word was with Jelly, and the Word was Jelly . . ." Like the old Logos, the new Logos is both mediator and incarnation, the jelling of what the world mostly experiences as polar incompatibles: absolute and relative, One and Many, objective and subjective, macrocosm and microcosm, the reality which lies behind "the veil of Maya" and the world of the *principium individuationis;* in sum, the principle of crucial relation and coherence, the clabber and retsin of things. Clearly this is not a wholly new Word, but one of the oldest, new only to a culture which has mostly forgotten the old modal themes and how to *live* them—the culture of Weismann's "mezzo-humanist chorus / . . . beating out shoes for plaster casts of deep-freeze Parthenon horses." What was once performed by religion is now no longer possible, for in this poem God is dead and the confessional abandoned ("The roof over the middle was gone, as if something inside had blown up, / Or something from outside had blown down.") The world to which Weismann, a secular "'forerunner'", tells the Word— though the world "comprehendeth it not"—is familiar enough; the world of fractured, atomized, hopelessly individuated things and men; in which baby-carriages conceal bazookas and the military budget corrupts the skies; where the great, naked, Greek sun blazes down on the puny humanists who worship the past but lack the personal jelly to live it; where the girls are transistorized, and nothing at all links the swallows "homing from Wyoming" and the bibliographer's unnatural passion; where the great junkyards of human culture celebrate death beneath the utterly unconnected Aurora Borealis, and the homosexual abortionist does his work behind the gash in the Clabber Girl billboard; where the oilman-cowboy hunkers toward his "gold-fluted bicuspidor", and the old American open road and the rollcall of the rivers are mocked by the rape and desolation of the land. It is quite a vision. And it is to this world where human life has somehow come unstuck from things, which has lost its retsin and jelly, that Weismann addresses his Word.

But if Weismann is no religious elegist fashionably mourning the loss of faith, he is also no modish academic apocalyptic delivering a secular Jeremiad on the decay of the times. True, the analysis is similar—the perversion of possibility, the corruption of nature, alienation, the cult of death and conformity in modern life—but there the resemblance ends. For Weismann believes that there *is* a jelly—the simple courage to live what one hopes for and believes, to have the courage of experience, to find a valid connection. The corrupt and the criminals of this poem are the timid, the self-corrupted, the unfree, the cowards—all those who lack the courage to live, to make a real jelly of their aspirations. Everybody really knows the Word, but most are "pragmatically deaf" and intent on drowning it out by whatever device—drugs, ambition, money, sex, or scholarship—they can contrive.

All great literature knows this quality—this bravery of life—of which Weismann is always essentially speaking. I think, for instance of the encounter between Glaukos and Diomedes in the *Iliad*. The Greek Diomedes, with full heroic courtesy, asks the Trojan Glaukos who he is and from whom descended, and Glaukos answers, sadly:

High-hearted son of Tydeus, why ask of my generation?
As is the generation of leaves, so is that of humanity.

The wind scatters the leaves on the ground, but the live timber
burgeons with leaves again in the season of spring returning.
So one generation of men will grow while another
dies. Yet if you wish to learn all this and be certain
of my genealogy: there are plenty of men who know it . . .

And then he proceeds, with utterly radiant inconsistency, to list, proudly and even joyously, the exploits of his famous line, from grandfather to father to son. In this one speech Homer gives us an emulsion as it were of the attitudes with which, between which, the hero must live. On the one hand is that obliterating, action-eroding view of things seen *sub specie aeternitatis,* taught by the spectacle of daily death, a view of human action as anonymous, fleeting and almost futile; on the other hand, an intense, enabling, tragic pride in human glory, a pride born of transience and made poignant by the long view. Somehow between these perspectives the hero lives, all his power and dignity deriving from his deftness in keeping both views in a vital suspension. What is held in suspension does not fall apart; what jells, coheres. Think too long on things *sub specie aeternitatis*—the perspectival vice of the Middle Ages—and you can easily become callous or indifferent, even cynical about mutable man; so too the Homeric gods, having only eternity to look forward to, can contrive neither meaning nor morality from their everlasting lives. The Homeric god is "laughter loving" because eternity and exemption from suffering have made him frivolous and shallow. Alternatively, one can become so involved in the present, so drugged by the dither of individuation and the social illusions of career and fame, that one lives in sustained falsehood and self-deception, in a timidity that kills. This, above all, is the obsessive danger of the modern world. It takes courage to cleave to the double vision, to give the Word by becoming Man oneself.

Everything I know of Donald Weismann as artist and man declares his involvement in this double vision. He is *par excellence* a man of suspensions, an emulsive man, striving to hold together, like eggwhite and oil in mayonnaise, past and present, real and actual—a man unusually hospitable to what is complex and demanding. At times I see in him all the crucial traits of the Homeric hero, a man vividly present, vividly angry, vividly generous and compassionate, above all courageous. Everything about him suggests a long modal meditation—a meditation which he finds fascinating as he finds its lessons intolerable. In his house in Austin the lampshades are made of old glass negatives: pictures of past generations building their houses *new,* once shiny new cars long since gone to junk ("a rain of junk on junk and rag and bone"), old styles, old birches long since chopped and burnt. The light by which he reads is thus purposely filtered through a film of other and past lives, a photographic shadow of mortality, and the whole proud splendid, modern house meanwhile outbraves, with children, dogs, cats, glass, and ease, all its treasured *memento mori.* As a painter, his latest, and perhaps his happiest, form is what he calls a photonegacollage: more glass negatives (he has thousands of them, almost all the work of an old Florentine maestro, bought in some junkshop for a few thousand lire), in which various objects—a head, an arm, a boat, etc.—are rubbed until they shine, giving them the effect of a nimbus or apparition, and then superimposed upon a mat of museum-tickets or sentimental postcards of gondolas or old spas or Raphael's *Disputa* or whatever. The result is a fresh emulsion of past and present, objective and subjective, the nightmare and the real—in short, "jellies" of remarkable composition and poignance, with the poise and suspension of true art.

These are Weismann's methods and perspectives and world: it is here that he lives. Both as man and artist, it is *incarnation* that he is after—moral and artistic poles in turbulent equipose; the life confirmed in the art, the art witnessed and asserted by the life. It is this identity of life and art that "Jelly was the Word" really declares. Modern culture, like modern man, is discontinuous because it lacks a single style, because men do not live their real convictions, because their works and beliefs are not records of their conduct. In this poem Donald Weismann, who practices what he preaches, tells of his own courageous odyssey as high-school teacher, hobo, sailor, university professor, and now general trailboss of the humanities at the University of Texas, and asks to be heard. He has earned the right. Listen . . .

—William Arrowsmith

Bread Loaf, Vermont

JELLY WAS THE WORD

Jelly, he said, and no one got the word,
Not even gooseflesh in the backdraft.

Jelly was the word as surely as
A fair ball batted backwards
Is foul.

The word was his to voice abroad
In hopes it could be heard by anyone
In certainty or doubt,
Dungarees or double-breasted pinstripes,
Robed in worms or cloth or naked
In wisdom or ignorance, stretching to marvel
The excarnation of the hooded false.

When the sun came out, stripped as Greek mythology in Basic Esperanto,
He formed the word full in the leeside air of a hill
Upstream so it would carry the load of tidings down
Almost according to the local weather prediction, and maybe
Get through to the most unsuspecting.
But those about were in mezzo-humanist chorus
With anvils, tongs and sledges
Beating out shoes for plaster casts of deep-freeze Parthenon horses
While singing to keep their ears pragmatically deaf.
He funneled the word down and lofted it on high,
But unhearing they went about their copyrighted schedule to noon
When they kidnapped a child in effigy, the daily ritual
For keeping the curriculum from jeopardy
And untowardness.

At five, by a timepiece ignited by a dead President
From the bowl of fire at the Olympics,
They queued up to a shake or trill and galloped behind
An overlapping spur,
While his last trumpeted jelly came hallooing back from the hills around,
Unsullied and unheard.

Yelling jelly into the wind, for who knows where
A dark-adapted protectively colored wayfaring intimate
May bend his ear,

He rode the rods below the oldest reefer of the Nickel Plate
To night in Cleveland's yard.

Where the tracks brake-shine under
The ferro-concrete arch named nineteen-oh-nine,
Big and square in a recessed panel,
He eased from his knees to the gravel
And headed beneath the bridges for the square below the tower
Built with a lot of hard arms and stolen bilk carried unclean
To the top in a hod with a perforated bottom
That failed to drain away the filth.

Night in the bilious grass of the square,
Criss-crossed with suicidewalks,
Sucked out bunches of hoarheads mixed
With the young defeated in their own success.
They stood around in slipknots wearing tin
Questionmarks arguing for no stakes between chewing.

In the stop-watched seconds when every body was silent,
Chewing or thumbnailing their far back teeth at once,
There was nothing but the weak din of the place
That could be sliced by voice easier than amber light the fog.
And in those seconds they stood between
Blank and tense, looking the same, but smelling different
To foxes and everything hunted.

Among them there was a brand of waiting
As if they'd been hurt in the gaps of their reason,
And to bridge the wound had found
A whipping-goat to flail with a swipple loaded with nails
And drive to trial for defecation of their undecipherable characters.

In this receptive blank, this
Waiting for waiting, no matter for what,
He who held the word could hope to have it heard,
So he told it through the din, then mushroomed it over the square
Like jelly inside the dome of the planetarium.

One wooden owl with mirror eyes planted
On a cornice of the courthouse
To scare away the chalk-loaded pigeons,
Tried to hoot as the word went out
Unheard, and its flock of echoes bleated away to din and died
As the silent chewing erupted again
In modulated belches and mouth muscle fussings that sounded
Something like but not language.

In a westbound cab driven with abandon
By a moonlighting high school English teacher worried sick
How he'd make ends meet and just barely,
He was carried carrying the word to a bottleneck east of Ashtabula

Where the sign said KNOW YOU TURN and the driver did,
Clear around to N. Y. U.

The last generation of the Institute's early Cinquecentists was returning
In an Albertian line from a coffee break in step
With footnotes on arches.
They'd given up the trace of man in paint and stone
Along with cigarettes and rhythm-method humanism,
Too troubled on the one hand by the possibility of abscess
Making the heart grow fonder, and on the other
By the harrowing possibility of flat-out confrontation
With the magnificent Italian dead-end.
Ex post facto architectural theory and oldtime unsymbolic logic
Are two slow fasts they kept to avoid the feast of those
They'd slaughtered in themselves.

They walked the radius of a circular park
After carefully stepping over the circumference,
And assembly-lined their way towards the center
Where he who had the word stood,
A physical block.
Knowing that these professing doctors without patience spoke,
And even understood many languages natively,
He pronounced jelly to them in the standard cultivated manners
Of every language, group and sub-family of

Indo-European, Semetic, Finno-Ugric, Dravidian,
Malayo-Polynesian, Turkic, Monogolic, Sino-Tibetan and even
Hokan out of Iroquoian
For that semester's guest in Advanced Etruscan Tub Vaults,
On leave from Princeton and Columbia.
It got into their pores, nostrils and navels,
Their ears, mouths and all aperatures south;
Their teeth, suet, bones and nails,
But it died there, all
Sundered and unheard.

Pushing down the narrow-gauge spasms of their constricted discipline,
They packed up so tight at the compass-pricked center where he stood
That they broke wee puffs of vestigal kamikaze, pre-soured
In the costic channels of their inner dark.

Outraged by the frustration of their one-track blight-of-way
To the second radius, that if traversed to the circumference
Would give them a whole diameter to their scholarly credit,
They dispatched the most compulsive of the squeezed
Out of the obfuscation to the Bell System to phone
For civil liberties.

The piewagon came full of New York's Finest in new jerseys.
The one with the longevity and double veteran's preference

Invited the word-carrying one inside and he asked why,
Only to be told that it looked like disorderly breach
In a public with no visible means, but
That was a matter for the bench.
When they began to push him in that way
That looks like overly demonstrative brotherly love from the outside,
But feels like valet service mixed with judo and sacked beebees inside,
A small boy with an olive slingshot standing on a hydrant
Said it would be false arrest because
One of the flatfeet was out of uniform, and
Quite suddenly he was released.

Freely bound, then, on his quest for a hearing ear, and giving
To the probability that the word might go forth better inside than out,
He hitched his hopes to a star going west, like
Columbus, but a little more south.
Near the Rio Guadalupe he unhitched and hiked
Through derrick-shaded cotton fields and grasslands studded
With saltlicks and horn-brimmed spectacles
On four legs walking,
Into Victoramus of the Lonesome Star.

There on the main street where it most likely would be
In a town squared off around the courthouse jail,
The bank stood looking like a camouflaged safe keeping guard

Over its assorted but negotiable insides.
Through the goldleaf-lettered, plateglass door he went
With an air conditioned by purpose to a rose marble room where
Cattlemen came to trade winds and stock their accounts
While mostly hitting the double-fluted gold bicuspidors.

In the fortune projected beyond Mercator for him, he arrived
To the fanfare of the empty room, and
Took position for unleashing the word
From silence.

While the 33⅓ R.P.M. platter of recorded electronic bell sounds
Played out the blinded arcades of the phoney
Belfry of the Refundamentalistic steeple,
Only to tell time what it already knew,
The cattlemen came dragging their kale behind them.
They hunkered down to trade and borrow
And write notes to the promissory land.
By nicatating and tonguing their cheeks they signalled
The branded hides to change range and hands
Across the taut barbed wire.

Without a sound among the hunkered and one,
Except the almost imperfectible tick
Of the time-lock on the Swiss-movement safe,

And the humming of the cowboy spitoon,
He pealed out the word
Gloriously free in the marble room.
The acoustics were chambered like a nautilus encouraging
The air to perfect vibrations of audible articulations
Corresponding exactly to the letters of the law
And the syllables of the word
Which should have exported the import
Through sensation to the hunkered, but
All that went returned converted to
Unregenerative feedback that bladdered his gall
As memory and not a call.
Undismayed, he mooed and snorted the word, and
Whinneyed and brayed it asslike around the cattlemen,
All to the same dissolute end.

As on every day in every week, except Sunday when
They played the other game with the lamb,
They went about their silent business in the marble room
As if alone without themselves, unconscious
Of what they did to pay or rob, but doing
It like ritual unconceived, half in dumb neglect
And half in awful vengeance.

The little click that crawled across the wall

Issued from the time-lock pinching tight for overnight,
Signalling the session's end.
Trading their last scents and dollaring up their accounts,
Like sleeves the ravelled care,
They amblingly unhunkered for the door.

Once more he intoned the word while the bought sold and slaughtered
Grazed or bled in grass or profusion far from their executors,
Free as stray swine in the county without a hogreeve.
The word splashed jelly on their shirt-fronts, bags of their pants,
Over their naked faces, spread on the ceiling and walls,
Then glacéd the marble floor.   Unheard.

Halfway to the filigree porch
He sensed an ideal accoustical balance between spaces
Open and closed like time ajar in the fruit cellar,
And he laid out the word in a horizontal wall
At the level of their departing ears.
It ran around the globe, an earlevel Heaviside layer laving
The pinna, meatus and tympanum,
Then splayed lost in the labyrinth.

Along the street paved with dust and darkness,
The evening paper came out biased at the seams precisely on time,
And he looked for the lost and found help-wanted personals

In the ads of the have-not.
No one, nor even a tax-whelped corporation,
Syndicate or extremely non-profit foundation garment
For the founder's unction bed was advertising a lust
Or a hunch for hearing.
So, wistfully, there on the dark corner
Where east meets west and north and south to boot,
He watched the kipling down of the town
Into no dreams it had not had.

In the morning,
A little back from Tillamook Bay
Near the pioneers' museum, a child
Playing with a plastic tongueblade and parts of a pop-up toaster,
Looked his way when he said jelly,
But his mother, harried and wary,
Pulled him back into a narrow coop where
A cock crew and something heavy fell.

One other light of recognition did flicker
In the opal eyes of a girl certified as mad
By a kind of pick-up band acting as a kangaroo court
One night near Natchez when things were dull, and all
The playing cards were stuck together with cruor.
She appeared to hear the word, and weakly

Rasped the dormant nerve a little, just before
Her spoils-system attendant cuffed her far left of crippled
And smothered her under an inner-spring mattress
Behind the tall unwindowed bars.

Where the red green and gold lay the deepest along the Olentangy,
Out beyond the beating drum-shaped stadium
And the cemetery begun as a Confederate prison,
He saw two lovers through a sycamore screen.
In the Saturday afternoon sun, with the town siphoned off
Into the million-dollar football bowl,
They lay there almost alone in Franklin County.
The breeze was from someplace filled
With honeysuckle, frankincense and murmur,
To which they added musk, a trace of fingerling and sighs
They shed their clothes and stabled their cares
And made each in the other's image inseparable,
Wrapped, spathed and spermed anaesthetized.
The moving shadows wrote them in the leaves
And they answered in the last of the sun.
They rose regenerate to a world still at their ease,
And while it held he floated out the word,
Only to pass around and through them;
A light unseen,
A time unkept.

36

Along his way to the coast
Where the memory of the old oaken Arkies still rapes the path,
He called the word up to a hole in a library facade
Where an Arizona grackle was
Being shot for lunch by a bibliographer.
As the bird fell into the awning below,
The bibliographer leaned out mumbling that:
The first copy, Celery King Collection, acquired from Mogol Flatt,
Is one of six known in original wrappers with all points
Plus inserted four-leaf clover, but reconstructed and
Spine title so pasted that it now heads up.

Just in case the bibliographer was using his mouth to repudiate his ears,
He called the word up the wall between breaths,
Only to have it pushed back with a recitation that:
The Jenny Wren Version is in original condition, possibly
Of black cloth as reported by Heartman and Canny,
And of an issue which,
Like those before and after,
Incorporates some no-name as well as Craghead and Slip titles, and
That if the report is unverified and the variant discovered
Only in green cloth it should be
Reclassified as 3b (issue 3, variant impression 3).

Some swallows homing from Wyoming flew south
While the bibliographer kept spewing his diarrhoeal down
The classicistic wall by incremental repetition,
And the man with the word walked away west
To the outskirts of Los Angeles.

There, before the expressway begins to be what it expressly is,
He paused at the hubcap crusted gate that gave
To a hundred-acre automotive Forest Lawn.
The sun was burning on the other side of the earth,
Blocked out by the crust, moho and molten core,
But the blackened sky behind the graveyard was caught in the crossfire
Of the Auroras Borealis and Australis and it flickered
Fitfully in a barrage of sheet steel lightning.
The once worshipped graveyard junk gave back
Chromium lights from the bloodpoisonous dark
Hovering close among the grease-cold unhooded heads,
Toothless flywheels flown dead into the back transmission cavity,
Fractured shock-absorbent arms, shocked their last by the lost road, hanging
Under the unhinged jaws of girder-booms in once one-piece frames and skeletons,
Litters now for exploded doors, undriven shafts, unsteered wheels galore;
Universals manifolded, bent twisted, cracked and broken waiting
The clarion call to shrapnel in the next somewhat limited war.
Here and there the angled iron was hung with upholstery crape moving
Ominously as Georgia Spanish moss in May

Through flake-edged saws of safety glass.
Between the closed-out open hearses, the oiled loam lay
Strewn with spring leaves and visors for the sun,
Bristling cold with brasted fuel-injection pumps,
Pistons, needle valves, gaskets, shims, handles, hinges
And non-armorial ballbearing escutcheons aping heraldry.

The moon went under and the rats peeked out;
They left their nests in dried-out liquid clutches
And collapsed synthetic seats still half stuffed
With plastic straw and crumbs, to search abroad for sustenance
And openings for fever, tuleramia, typhus, rabies and plague.
To the north an angelus sounded three and three and nine,
Then nine and three and three undoing.

Through the gate he went along the rutted way of delivery and salvage,
Far to the back against a cyclone-fenced hill
Where a blacked-out cut-rate pay-as-you-go abortion clinic was
Operating full-blast in practiced caution.
The German shepherd, asleep full of rats, was chained to a generator
Fitted with an obliterated brand-name in red and fleur-de-lys.
There were little sighs from inside the tin sign lean-to,
And something like ozone from shock treatments in the air.
The television program, on base in the cubical filled with waiting,
Was moving in six near-middle grays

Backed up with muted juke-Bached catechism preludes
While the well-tempered cleaver and absorbent cotton worked
In the padded induction room beyond.

He cast his eyes through a gash in a Clabber Girl sign,
Past the polyethylene sink to the war-surplus hospital unit inside
Where the work was being done on an olive drab rack.
The one in charge in a barber's coat had been a triple-threat man,
Voted All-American Second Team, the first ever
From the College of the Maculate on its drive
To national recognition and fiscal solvency.
He'd not been good enough for pro-ball, so he'd tried insurance
Until he heard about visions from the printed testimony
Of a State's Evidence Witness against a Harvard graduate
Accused of aiding and abetting the red homonculus.
Helped by an old head injury inflicted during a homecoming game years before,
He drank himself to his own sure-fire vision, realized
In a rebuilt Trailways bus with enormous tent and Hammond organ,
Driven, pitched and played to evilangelize from border to border until death
By strangulation of his male organ player cost him all
His new gained wealth, reputation as a healer,
And eight years in the pen.
His pen-pals advised the junk-pusher's trade, but once out,
He turned, rather, to this graveyard procuring of premature delivery.

Now, framed in the gash and obviously at the end of the night's agenda,
He was washing and wringing his hands in the sink.
Then, still with the towel, he collapsed
Into the tubular chair at the plastic-topped table and dropped
His head on his folded arms with an agonizing groan.

In the consummate silence that resumed, and musing
How the stars at noon come out from the bottom of the pit,
The man with the word voiced it clearly through the gash in the tin.
It went straight home to the one in the barber's coat
And he rose up in stark naked fright, there
At the end of his camouflaged nightmare.
While his drums still beat with the waves of the word,
And the one who'd given it backed away from the wall,
He reached for the desperate ace in the panic hole
And pushed the button of his last but one resort.

The circuit, by his final unfree act,
Ringed through the trigger to the charge
Of the nine-pound fragmentation bomb,
And for an instant between none and after-image,
Incandescence bloomed in a corner of the graveyard,
Then gave the vacuum back to the rush of darkness
In a rain of junk on junk and rag and bone.

Only the rats far out from the epicentrum
Squealed a requiem in life,
And a toad or a dog, someplace,
Strained out an erotic chord.

The one with the word looked away from nothing
Toward the tar-seamed road where the trucks run east,
Lighting the pole-tops and canyon floors
All the winding way to mile-high Denver.

There, after breakfast, he stood on the shoulders of a regential statue,
In situ at the intersection of every concrete path leading
To every clock-wired classroom of an accredited university.
He watched the old children, female and male,
Follow the drawing-board lines like fenced troughs
To their sheep-dip catalogue-described eight o'clock classes.
The deodorized girls were dressed in magazine photographs open down the front,
Carrying their transistor books and pancake bags casually
As they walked caressing themselves in nylon sandwiches out of sight.
The boys, bereft now of subsidized juvenile delinquency, and adrift
Between recollections of pre-puberty and cart-blanche anticipation,
Were thumbing their way to the suck-in of some organizational claque
Where, relieved of responsibility for their acts, should they dare,
Could some day soon dandle the oscillations of their erotomania

On an expense account while doing what's necessary only
To provide statistics in support of a long deceased fiction.

The grass had been cut and rolled by tandem power mowers,
The brick and stone courses tuck-pointed that spring;
The windows were washed and shaded adroitly with pastel blinds,
All under a fleece-wisped sky so deep and high
It took more than the naked eye to find the vapor streaming
Behind the military budget, just before the sonic booms.

From this high place of vantage, straddling the close-spaced ears
Of the regent unremembered though cast in bronze way before the day he died,
The one with the word filled his lungs with the colloquial
Air of the place and broke forth the word through the unexpecting hum.
Its crested waves were seismographic and little inked needles around the world
Charted the duosyllable jelly, just so, on paper rolls and drums.
But its sound, if to them at all, lay on the land
Like the sound of a bell made of meat.

With no more adieu than the day is lost going west
Across the line on the other side of the Great Plains beginning,
They went their sequestered ways, some to bingo-jargon games played with ponies
And some few to non-sequiturial lectures full of perspectives by incongruity.
At ten minutes to nine precisely, and by a Pavlov bell multiplied,
They made the doors and steps back to the concrete belts, and on

To the half-circle clearing under the Tudor windows of the Vice President
Where they demonstrated, minuet-like, about certain campus parking restrictions.

The mousey faculty judges, appointed by the paranoic dean,
Sat after an engraving of Raphael's *Disputa* on a balcony hung over
The exactly prescribed student demonstration area,
To score by points on square tagboard grids, easily fitted to the lap,
The comparative degrees of decorum as defined
In the regentially prepared and newly re-tied Hand and Foot Book for Students;
And as manifested by the various Greek letter groups
Of the Pan-Hellenic Society during this particular demonstration
Now ending on time, four minutes before nine.

The winning group, a sorority whose strategy had been passive assistance,
Was present only by proxy in the person of the sorority father, who
Happened, also, to be the paranoic dean.
He was outrageously applauded by his self-appointed judges
As they presented to every member of the sorority, in absentia,
A gold-stamped, top-grained cowhide slip-on cover
For their personal prints of the Hand and Foot Book.
After the Pan-Hellenic hymn was sung, and a maintenance man on the roof
Ran the Decorum Flag up to the soft underside of Old Glory,
The President of the Senior Class led them in collective unconscious meditation,
While the vines quietly clawed their way up the wall.

From his perch on the dead regent's bronze pate,
In the still of twenty-seven seconds to nine,
The man with the word loosed it loud again and then attended
The echoe's funeral procession all along the ring around
The Rockies' pocket full of mile-high Denver.

Somewhere in cellars or bunkers far back and under,
Some other students may have been plotting toward truthfulness,
But their retreats kept out as well as in,
So what they did and said was as dead without
As jelly was within.

Over a ridge where a path falls down in Maryland,
The man with the word angled his way to Camp Pinkerton,
Named for Allan the cooper who foiled the Molly Maguires, and
Kept Old Abe from being shot until Booth did it in a box
And Allan's sons went a-scabbing in May with labor spies.

The pup and top-dog tents were neat in row on row,
(Oh gently down the scream with a PX whisky wash),
Well away from the officers' mansions covered
With masonry hors d'oeuvres and rank flags flying
In the slipstream of another smokescreen investigation,
Involving low candlepower in the mess hall and shower,
Trumped up to wet-blanket the red-hot charges

Of brutality to the literates refusing to use in time of peace
The toilet articles of war.

Hard by the electric picket fence, where
A sign shouted out PEACE IS OUR PROFESSION—SLEEP WELL TONIGHT,
The motor pool stood shimmering with rockets
Rigged up as bookmobiles and ambulances.
The half-track bicycles, bought on a southern contract just before election,
Were lined up smart before the amphibious baby carriages
Loaded with gesundheit bazookas and four-in-hand grenades.
The high flung command cars with mohair seats were back
From a Colonel-and-up safari in New Nations Africa,
With side trips to the Western Indies and ex-French Asia,
And they lined the mall through the center of the pool
Draped with trophies and form letters from off-Central Intelligence.
Between the ram-jam radiation bulldozers, uncontaminated earth spreaders,
Troop-dropping trucks and mobile missile planters, a Private First Class
Was reaming the tail-pipes free of carbon vacuously
When the man with the word hissed jelly through the fence.
The Private kept reaming as if dreaming of the metaphors
He was mixing, and pointed blank to the mess hall yonder.

The siren way up the water tower bewailed the loss of morning,
And half a division of non-commissioned flowers of youth
Anthologized at the steam tables of their mid-day meal.

At the decibel height of the uncushioned mess hall clatter,
When seven and half thousand were in a single sight,
The cocky chicken-Colonel appeared in starch and brass at the open front door,
Flanked by two West-Pointed Majors and a pair of VMI Captains to keep the score,
He cued-in the command that wracked the hall in tiers of attention
And laid away the last living sound in the fresh-created mausoleum.
Into this erectilinear solid of silence, and before the next regular command,
The man with the word sent it forth in a blast of sound that resounded
From every atom in every molecule of solid, liquid and gas.
But the half-division of men with a full division of ears
Stood as a single frozen stone,
Numbed deeper into dumbness by blind respect and fear
Of the uniformed team-shaped myth, mythically champing at a glorious bit.

He left Camp Pinkerton while the shadows were still underfoot, and overhead
An orinthopter owned by a Puerto Rican ad agency, trailed a fretwork sign
That read EMIT NWO RUO NI EVOL SI YTIRUCES LAICOS from the north,
And from the south: SOCIAL SECURITY IS LOVE IN OUR OWN TIME.

That night, between the tarnished gold coast and the flaming skies of Gary,
He watched the thousands go in guilt-edged boredom,
Curiosity, ignorance and emptiness
Down the streets and through the concrete holes
Into Chicago's Soldier Field,
To see and hear Young Billy Migraine,

The crusading self-evaginist, go vertigo and hypnotize
Half a hundred thousand with himself on snow bird snuff,
About a no-down-payment Jesus who consecrates the status quo.

Thinking of great numbers and the scatter of probability for almost anything,
The man with the word filed in with the mob to a seat on the fifty-yard line.
High on the rim of the Field, under the moonless sky by the lake,
He watched Young Billy career in his checkered coat and movie face,
Right down to the semi-final when he called
For a hundred thousand safety matches to be lit
To prove his light in mob psychology darkness.
And while the matches burned in something like noiselessness,
The man with the word thundered it out, then shrieked it staccato;
But not a match died out, nor was a voice borne high or low
Until Young Billy Migraine called for personally autographing Jesus
To the music of electric guitars.

The sky threw up, and the man with the word
Went by a side gate to the open road
Past places that still await their names,
To Billings on the Yellowstone.

Along the river where the outcropping prehistoric remains,
A Memphis gambling outfit was working hard in its carnival guise
To get to Great Falls in the clear.

The snag-numbered wheels and skin games with five-sided bones
Were slicing the deficit when a Blackfoot and a Kootenai, too suddenly fleeced,
Lashed the debonair concessionaire to the other side of his birthday
With smartly matched lacings from straps of plaited thong and horsehair.
The man with the word had witnessed it all,
So the Billings police took him off to one side
To get his statement of what had happened before and after the brawl.
Tell us, they said, in your very own words, how it went pell-mell to melee;
And the man said he needed only one to tell, and that one was jelly.
The Sergeant said he'd better be careful, sir,
About withholding an officer and resisting evidence,
But the man kept answering with jelly, loud and clear,
Until the Sergeant took his fingerprints and turned him over to the State Patrol.
In their souped-up Mercury with automatic guns in the upholstery they told him,
By damn, he sounded like one of those liberals from Eastern Montana State Normal,
So forthwith they sped him into the Bitterroot Range
And dumped him hard in a gray ghost town.

On a raft of shingles, clapboards and saloon doors,
He floated away from Three Forks, down the Missouri,
Across the plains of North and South Dakota,
Nebraska, Kansas, Iowa and Missouri, calling jelly all the way
Along the river and into Bismark, Pierre, the City of the Sioux,
Council Bluffs, Omaha, Atchison, Leavenworth and Kansas City, clear
To the Father of Waters, seventeen miles above Saint Louis.

He beached his raft where the waters meet and watched them prove they were one.
With a brush of river rushes and paint of the brightest clay,
He lettered out the world as a sign on the darkened raft
And stood it against an oak growing gray in the waters' Y.
He walked the tufted banks below the bluffs, the sands
Along the coming peneplain, past the bridges spanning east,
South out of the west to Looey's name-sainted City of the Blues.

He turned with the town away from the river and the castiron-gated fronts
Into streets the flatboatmen and sidewheel trade helped
To plank and cobble below the tar and cement.
A piano was being played by a half-gone son of the Proclamation
Stilted up on a dunnage stand behind the handwrought bar,
Under the neon lights jumping in a jack-knife dive on Rummage Street.
The melody was anchored in rhythmic pitch that kept the flukes from rusting,
And by the chain she rocked the vessel through the doors of the lock
Between the high morning river and the low down twilight blue.

The man with the word took a table near the door
And felt the pulse pushing up through the floor.
He opened his mouth in the shape of the word,
But before the night air in him could come out to say,
The bartender nodded and pointed that way.

By a force not quite his own, and stronger it seemed,
He rose from the table and went where he'd been pointed.
There in the back where the backroom boys could be having a ball,
A painter was painting at a converted confessional.
With his feet planted wide apart, he worked on a canvas
Nailed to the flat back of the dead magic stall.
The roof over the middle was gone, as if something inside had blown up,
Or something from outside had blown down.
The one-way cloth to left and right was rent away by time and breath,
The swinging doors, unswung, revealed the worm-holey seat, filled
With fidgets and little dark spots as deep as the plank.

The man with the word stood at the corner where easel and confessional met,
And, staring at the border of end and beginning, drew a deep breath.
But instead of the word, a great block came and constipated the man with pain;
He fell to the floor and rolled, kicked and thrashed and moaned,
While the painter, painting still, eased him around to the easel side
Where, in the light of the backroom glow, the painting showed.

The man with the word looked up from the pulsing floor,
Into the yellow-gold, white on black vermillion, green to blue and
Clear through the placeless space filled with images moving, never still,
Full of the tides of eyes and seas, the weather of rocks and bones,
An infinite field in a single flower of life-as-life continuous.

There on that piece of canvas, the painter's sudarium, was wiped afresh
The color of lost surprize, the face of first encounter.
There the infinitely distanced multitudes and varieties were patterned
In a life-size sensuous replica of the fated everlasting force
That winds and binds absolute and relative in wordless space and time.
And the man who called it by the name of jelly, lost the word like the ghost
As the block gave way and the pain flew with the sight.

Far off a wooden owl on a cornice of a courthouse hooted,
A child felt warm in a coop a little back from Tillamook;
Flowers bloomed in an innerspring mattress in Natchez, while a bell
Tolled one among the Los Angeles graveyard junk,
And a word on a raft blew down in the rivers' Y.

1000 Copies of
JELLY WAS THE WORD
Published December, 1965
by
The Pemberton Press
Austin, Texas